PRACTICE AND SCIENCE OF RELIGION

PRACTICE AND SCIENCE OF RELIGION

A STUDY OF METHOD IN
COMPARATIVE RELIGION

BY

JAMES HAUGHTON WOODS

GYAN

Published by

GYAN

Gyan Publishing House
5, Ansari Road
Daryaganj, New Delhi-110002
Phone: 011-47034999, 9811692060
E-mail: books@gyanbooks.com

Distribution Network
gyanbooks.com
India, USA, Canada, UK, Australia

ISBN: 978-93-6208-649-5 (HB)
First Published, 1906

2nd Impression 2024

Printed at: Gyan Press, Delhi.

PRACTICE AND SCIENCE OF RELIGION
Author: JAMES HAUGHTON WOODS

PRACTICE AND SCIENCE OF RELIGION

THE PADDOCK LECTURES

1905–1906

PRACTICE AND SCIENCE OF RELIGION

∴

A STUDY OF METHOD IN COMPARATIVE RELIGION

BY

JAMES HAUGHTON WOODS

INSTRUCTOR IN PHILOSOPHY AT HARVARD UNIVERSITY

LONGMANS, GREEN, AND CO.

91 AND 93 FIFTH AVENUE, NEW YORK

LONDON AND BOMBAY

1906

TO THE MEMORY OF

JOHN COTTON SMITH

AND

HARRIETTE APPLETON SMITH

IN GRATITUDE AND

REVERENT AFFECTION

PREFACE

These lectures were delivered at the General Theological Seminary in New York during January and February of this year. The general topic assigned for the lectures was Comparative Religion. My interest in this subject, persistent for many years, was first aroused by the Paddock Lecturer for 1882, a man who stimulated all my ideals, who revealed to me the charm of the scholar's life, and who bound my life to his in loyal admiration forever. To him I have ventured to dedicate this work.

The general method which I have followed and tried further to develop I owe to lectures of Kaftan; to work under Harnack in several successive seminars; and last of all to personal suggestions from Windelband, in lectures and on delightful strolls up the valleys of the Vosges. With classes at the university, my treatment of the subject has adapted itself to the men with whom, from year to year, I have studied the Science of Religion. The religious traditions of these men are divers; but Jews and mystics, Buddhists and Vedantists, are one with Christians and agnostics in their desire to find common ground. The search for points of contact between different religions has been encouraged in every way; points of contrast have often seemed more superficial, and obvious enough.

In this same spirit these lectures are given to the search for positive ground common to many religions. To some persons, however, this undertaking must inevitably seem negative in its aim, since the unique qualities of religions are not brought into the centre of discussion. In an informal address, which the students at the Seminary were good enough to ask me to give, I explained what positive results may be expected if the ground common to different religions be sought with the candour and the thoroughness required. One religion influences another best when it has enough confidence in itself to take the point of view of the other before attempting to shift that point.

An illuminating paper on Rinzai by Dr. Motora has been extremely useful to me. It is a pleasure to remember the generous advice and patient correction of manuscript by Mr. B. Preston Clark and by my brother. And I wish especially to thank many new friends at the Seminary for the hearty welcome to their midst and for much sympathetic criticism.

Cambridge, Massachusetts
March 21, 1906

CONTENTS

LECTURE FIRST

I
NEW AND OLD SCIENCE OF RELIGION

A Hundred years ago, when our forefathers were founding theological seminaries, the science of religion, far from needing to justify its existence, dominated all our life, our morals, our art and even our philosophy of nature. Natural theology, as our fathers then called it, was the predominant creative activity; its foundation was fixed; its career seemed indubitably sure. But its importance proved to be transitory; the generation which followed found all theology irksome and trusted itself to Sir Walter Scott and to the worship of beauty. Such aesthetic reforms do away with narrow antagonisms, and fill men with eagerness and delight, with personal enthusiasms, and with larger outlooks. Any age, capable of such experiences, capable of loyalty to ideals of beauty, must regard abstract teachings with impatience, and easily falls into the habit of counting austere theology a useless and offensive anachronism. Nevertheless a thoroughly modern science of religion has its own right to existence, has its own ends, less ambitious perhaps, but of distinct significance; precisely as a modern ethics, however different from the old English hedonism, has, as ever, its own ends to-day. These ends, however, can no longer be attained by the procedure of the old systems. As the problems of life have changed with changing conditions, so likewise the methods. To-day, neither in art nor in ethics nor in religion can we start with abstractions; to-day we can no longer by dialectics deduce religion from metaphysics. Like art and morals, religion must be appreciated as a personal experience; it must be approached not as a half-transcendental existence, but as real life, as a human interest, as an actual affair not far from any one of us. It must be viewed from the individual case, with the fewest possible assumptions, with the candour which pervades the laboratory,—so only can there be any hope of recovering the ancient trust in a science of religion.

This situation is not peculiar to religion: it is true of medicine; it is true of mathematics. All the mental presuppositions of our days are shifting, we are beginning to feel the extent of these changes. Many of us are amazed at their intricacy. They are the changes which follow our successes; and they are changes not only in the methods of the sciences, but in the whole range of our perceptive powers. We are stimulating our sensitiveness to a degree beyond our capacity for dealing with the results of our perceptions. It is not easy for us to master our impressions: we crave excitement, we need judgement. Our need is the ability to control everything we get in terms of ordered values. Mere impressions produce a tremendous commotion which dies away and leaves little result. Impressions, if new, cause rapture for a time and then disappear. Capacity to follow our own plan must prevail, if we are to keep impressions at all. There must be a scheme, some kind of order; there must be a sense of levels; there must be the perception of an end, even if the spontaneity of life seem less. So the discovery would follow that order is not, as the modern mind easily persuades itself, a tyranny, but rather the only freedom.

In our patriotic speeches we pay all honour to ideals of liberty: we ask, with almost romantic desire, perfect freedom for ourselves. For less fortunate peoples who have been thrown into contact with us, we are equally sure that nothing is so wholesome as discipline. The explanation might be that liberty often suggests to us nothing more than the ability to act without regard to consequences; and others, we think, need discipline not to help them to act, but because they prevent us from doing as we wish. We refuse others liberty because we have not disciplined ourselves. Accordingly liberty and discipline bring disorder each to the other in proportion as we try to divorce them.

In art, also, we are not satisfied with austere typical forms such as could express, with beautiful precision, the common ideals of a whole Greek city. These forms expressed a sense of order, embodied a clear purpose, and steadied each man's life. To us they seem unreal, remote from actual business, too dispassionate, too impersonal. We choose, instead, vivid expressions of sudden changes of feeling or of some wayward mood, varying with our personality, varying even with the emotional oscillations of a single day. Is it as easy for us as for the Athenian to enjoy the overtones, to trace the values which interweave the work with social order or with religious standards? Do we not oftener require intense experiences of single souls, less limiting conditions, less implications, more of vibrating life, more actual rhythms of passion?

We have, it is true, learned to approach our art with more freedom, with more candour, with more delight; but have we gained the ability to add to the impression the power to reach an appreciation, to test the value of the capricious taste, to add to the pure delight the more permanent satisfaction of an orderly adjustment to life?

Religious ideals are likewise in process of modification. All classes of persons, poets, critics, journalists and philosophers, are restlessly searching for personal beliefs. Unattached to any religious body, they are discussing earnestly, with a new range of sensitiveness, the foundations of belief and hitherto unperceived shades of religious meaning in life. The emphasis is personal; and the result is a swelling stream of vivid religious impressions and expectations.

Still more significant is the change in the whole religious mood of our day and of our time. It is not easy to describe or to trace this mood, unless it be said that it has broken forth, by the law of contrast, from the depths of the human soul. But it is a fact that we have become averse to self-discipline in preparation for a world to come, to programmes of salvation, and to tables of virtues and vices. Our occupation is to master this world now, to test it in actual personal experience, and by our own vigour and skill to sift out its defects and diseases and add to its beauty and its sanity.

This personal mood might well have been transitory and insufficient. But it has proved to be permanent and well ordered, and has become one of the main ingredients in what is called Modern Science. This habit of mind has overwhelmed the ancient world. Its method has been to search for as many fresh sensations and values as possible; to arrange all fresh insights into life in orderly series; to test the whole and the parts by a personal verification which shall be unfaltering and final. In such wise, this mood has mastered Nature, has overcome the distrust of Nature, and has put the keys of authority over Nature into the hands of the exultant individual. Modern expressions of belief, with few exceptions, are striving to adjust themselves to this new authority. New and alien personal impressions are invading the ancient order. Ideals of personal behaviour, of hygiene, of technical arts, of law and of charity are already ordered upon the new plan. Every newspaper recognizes the new authority, and each school is kneading the minds of the coming generation into the new scientific moulds.

The new sense of order, which is Modern Science, makes certain insistent personal demands upon modern religion. It does not make a religion; it adjusts the expressions of the religious life to the new order. Religion can well exist with no orderly methods from any scientist; and science thrives without religion; but theology presupposes both.

And the Science of Religion of to-day is the attempt to give a new order, and as these lectures will try to show, a new sense of correspondence between the intensely personal experiences of religion and the social or mystical experiences of religion. It assumes the point of view of the observer. Like any other science it attempts to order impressions and values. It has no intention of creating a religion; just as the chemist has no intention of creating an element or the historian a charter. Its method is the same as theirs. It differs from other sciences in that its material is not the same. This material is the beliefs and values of the religious life in all their known variations.

Science of Religion, then, is one of the most recent expressions of the modern type of mind. And the reason why it is more recent and more backward than other sciences seems to be altogether an historical reason.

The Christian Church was already becoming a compact and manageable unit when it first encountered the science of the Greeks, the only science of its day. The Church and the sinking civilization of the Roman Empire met as strangers. Unfortunately, instead of discovering that, in spite of differences in tradition, in outlook, in resources and in character, they were meant to live together, they gradually fell into a kind of pact, by which they agreed to remain apart, to make concessions, and then only on some few points to become more like each other.

Like every other religion, the Christian religion was at its beginning unfamiliar with science. The population in which it expanded was uneducated. The religion consisted in an almost ecstatic enthusiasm for a moral leader and for a divine kingdom. The enthusiasm for the Divine King and for the ideal society fused into one. The result was a new motive. This motive was a love which swept far beyond the limits of self, and resulted in a conquest of the soul; the charm of this conquest was subtle enough to be its own reward. There was no need of any other authority than this motive and its own operations. Still less were scientific evidences required. For the one flaming desire to reach souls was sufficient in itself. The generation which followed was of weaker moral fibre. Men asked others to choose for them courses of action when their own consciences alone should have given the decision. Singly these men could not face the pagan world; they must feel that they faced the world as members of an organization. The regulations which they received became the faith of the later Church; all else was profane. The contrast of the organized system of Christian beliefs and the outer pagan standards became permanent. God spoke in the Church; the thoughts of the world lacked the divine wisdom. But gradually the Pagans brought their ideals with them into the Church. They brought with them their science. For the most part this science was a tradition going back to Aristotle. He had taken into the physical world a principle of explanation which Socrates had used in the moral world. Socrates had been sure that things have their purpose in the moral world; Aristotle had used this moral purpose in the physical world as a principle of Nature. Man is a moral force;

Nature is a moral force; body is explicable as the moral purpose of soul. The snail's soul creates his body; his soul loves convolutions and so builds a body. The soul of the fish loves water and constructs an instrument to satisfy a moral need. Nature, likewise, is an instrument of the moral soul of Nature. But at that time this main scientific ideal of the pagan world was scarcely able even to transmit itself. The Stoics made some advances in ethics; but neither ethics nor science was an observation of experience; it was traditional; it was not more than a readjustment of the old principles to actual life.

This kind of science, dependent upon a moral force as its efficient principle, was the only science which the Christian Church knew. The Church felt no inclination and possessed no ability to produce for itself an independent science. It accepted the science, such as it was, of the schools. And after the first feeling of repulsion the tension soon ceased. It appeared that both Pagan and Christian were seeking a life differing from their own, the life of God, as both called it; each knew by experience that human life can find the connection with this larger life. The truth which both recognized was in the religious and ethical world. Both were sure of the final triumph of the spirit over the unmitigated life of the senses. Nature was for both a screen. They were to renounce all temporary desires, all care for trivial things; and they were to refashion themselves in their ideals. The sole use of knowledge was to enable each to distinguish what was true in this experience from what was plausible. Scientific truth was the discovery of ideals in life and was diametrically opposed to what truth might appear at first sight.

With this common end in view they came closer into touch than they were aware. But the Church clung to its first statement: the Church contains the absolute truth, the Pagan's religion is a feat of human reason unaided by divine knowledge. The pagan word "religion" and the pagan conception "religion," (in the sense that religion is every kind of practice which has as its end the pleasing or the appeasing of the gods,) were unknown to the Church. Thus the Church ignored the religious element in the Pagan's world, or, rather, counted that religion a philosophy and in no sense a demand of a people upon its God for life.

As a result of this situation, a concept of science extraordinarily important in the history of Western thought came into acceptance; science contains moral elements, but does not proceed from a revelation. Natural knowledge of God has nothing to do with religion in the fullest sense. This science is a production of man. If this science be called natural religion, it is after all imperfect religion. The nature of this compromise became clear as soon as the Western Church found itself confronting an entirely new and contemporary science. The aim of science was altogether changed. No longer was it an ethics with a cosmic background. It rested on two new kinds of personal experience: historical criticism and experimental natural science. At the same time mystics like Francis of Assisi or like Dante, although within the Church, made it appear that intense personal exaltation raised them above the world into the immediate experience of God, even when they were not in accord with the authorities. Thus the new individualism of science and of the mystics gradually upset the balance between natural and revealed religion.

The old science had lasted unquestioned for a thousand years. It lost first its ethical character; it interpreted nature irrespective of human desire, or of good and evil; it adopted experimental methods; it returned to atomic theories. Finally a new metaphysics appeared; no longer the product of myth and ethics and logic, but more and more a fresh unification of personal experience. But unlike the old Greek metaphysics, which had been the basis of natural religion throughout the Middle Ages, this new metaphysics did not rest upon any religious assumptions worth mentioning. Thus, only in quite modern times the way has been opened for a scientific treatment of religion. This Science of Religión is no longer natural religion with the old assumptions; it is now an historical and psychological classification of religious facts. It is the investigation and explanation of the religious life; it investigates and explains religious life as one investigates and explains morals, social forms or politics.

From this point of view Christianity is one of the religions; it is understood as one among many, or even as a part of a whole. The distinction between natural and supernatural, between revelation and reason, becomes of minor importance. More exactly, there would be in every religion both these elements: a natural element, in the old sense, the actual condition of the human animal unmodified by social needs or by ideal hopes; and, quite as truly, there would be in every religion a supernatural element, the activity which raises the human soul above the unabashed life of nature into a world of spiritual values, into a world which strives against stupidity and inertia and vulgarity.

The problems of this science would then be to collect, to order, and to estimate the facts: to discover what has been the direction of development, to ask what is the goal of this development, and to inquire whether the ideal goal exists in the development itself. Such a science is becoming, more and more, the basis for future systems of theology. If the programme could be carried out, the difficulties arising from practical treatment of a theoretical problem would diminish. Men engaged in the actual living of the religious ideals would afflict themselves less with the old enigmas: how to state miracles in terms of science; how Christianity maintains preëminence over all other religious forces; how a modern religion, which spurns the earthy and carnal, can yet dominate a modern civilization and a modern morality. These problems would not be solved, but they would become less oppressive. At the same time science would be less trammelled by personal feelings; theology would gain in candour and in authority; and religion would begin to feel the freedom of asserting its absolute character.

In some such way as this it would become much easier to be sure that religion is the experience of the presence of a larger life, necessary and universal, inclusive of all collective and personal forms of life. The basis of this experience would be the soul's desire for the permanency of its moments of complete insight; the experience itself would be the sense of a single inclusive purpose in human life; and the result would be the freedom to interpret its own individual share in that purpose. This sense of personal freedom, this certainty of the permanent values in one's own self, is a product of no science or theology; and no science or theology can destroy it. It is a fact of the personal life; one has it or has it not. But science can search for its simplest forms, can illustrate its connections with other expressions of life, can trace its intricate changes in history and estimate the worth of its different forms. Science can clear our minds of conflicting prejudices; it can convince us of the persistence of values in consciousness more inclusive than our own. It creates no fact; but it can form each man's impressions into a world; it can order beliefs into a total system of belief. An action adjusted to the belief in an inclusive system of beliefs is a religious act. Similarly our bodies act with reference to an external world, a projected system of sensations. Our world, whatever it may be, would be, without such inclusive systems, as if it did not exist. Our world is maintained, in each of us, only by our belief in an inclusive consciousness; it is maintained only by an unconquered effort to discover and to order purposes, beliefs and values.

This constant readjustment of personal impressions to a single standard is our religious experience. Our religion is the final purpose with regard to which we measure and use all of our impressions. This purpose is never passive. It is an act of will. The way to strengthen the sense of ordered values and beliefs in this will is to direct it in the right way, by interesting ourselves in the things which really matter. With this deep sense of the importance of discovering what things count, we begin, unconsciously it may be, to set up permanent systems of beliefs and values for ourselves, for human lives, for more inclusive lives.

These scales, expressed in terms of consciousness, are our religions. The Science of Religion is an artificial device to collect these experiences, and to aid in the process.

LECTURE SECOND

II

LEVELS OF VALUE

THE concentration of attention in science is not the same as the concentration of attention in religion. In science the observer is interested in the impressions and in their relations to each other, and is disinterested in himself. In religion there is interest in the person himself; the interest in the impressions has value only so far as it aids the assertion of the self in contrast to the world, only so far as it aids a man to count himself as a whole. This desire to contrast himself to his world is no fancy of his idle moments. It is as strong in his science and in his morality as in his religion. In his science he constructs a system of objective knowledge; he projects an image of an external world. In his morals he strives for a world wherein his ideal of good becomes real in action. But in religion he seeks satisfaction for himself as a whole from the universe as a whole. Often his science assures him that he is nothing more than a tiny group of oscillating energies; often his ideal good leaves him in doubt whether the good itself is more than a fascinating illusion. From these scientific and moral points of view he cannot escape the question, more or less constant, whether any effort of intellect or of self-sacrifice can preserve the individual life when confronted by Nature; whether his whole personality is not the product of forces accidentally combining without any end in view; whether all the learning and all the devotion of men will not, after all, prove to be futile labour.

It is religion which has helped to answer these questions in such wise that the feeling of self as a whole is not destroyed or narrowed. Even in the least civilized minds, and in its least sufficient forms, it is religion which gives men most freely the feeling of the value of personalitics. This is true when the self is contrasted with the chaos of living impressions which is the world to the mind of the savage; but it is true quite as well when the self is contrasted to the prim unearthly abstraction which is the world to the intellect of the physical scientist. This accomplishment gives religion its value; and this value is indispensable to the feeling of personality as a whole. The concept of the god represents, in a vivid symbol, the assurance in the heart of his worshipper that personality shall not be completely ignored in conflict with the world. The god encourages men, even when they are scarcely yet the physical match of the carnivorous animals, to impose upon nature the values of good and of evil; and he gradually helps to set men free to criticise Nature, or even to create worlds for themselves. Thus faith in a god is a declaration of superiority to the blind forces which dominate man's physical life.

The idea of the god, then, is the expression of the living relation which can bind together a man's world and his ideal of himself as a complete person. The idea of the god, in the form of symbolic imitations, or of rituals of purification, or of prayers, points out the way to the worshipper's ideal personality. The god assures to the worshipper the right to feel a contrast to the world, and the right to feel a correspondence to something more inclusive and higher than man's present momentary self. And this sense of the values of personality is not a mere postulate or a meaningless mystery; it is an intense form of the love of life. The mystery lies quite as much in the nature of life itself as in any of the expressions of life; and the postulate has its basis wherever life manifests activity.

Each religion searches for higher correspondences to

life; this search may be for bodily satisfactions, or for fulfilment of social desires, or for values of beauty and of conduct,—so far as any of these aims make a man surer of self, and develop his individuality, his criticism of life, or his power of judgement. Impressions are ranked with reference to the sense of expansion of self or of contraction of self. Each religion has its own scale of values, and differs in its sense of the value of personality and in its search for higher correspondences. Accordingly, each religion differs in its idea of its god, since the god is the expression of its own standard of values for the whole of life. The gods of each religion are therefore symbols of an inner sense of successful contact between the whole personality and the world.

So long as judgements of value are merely special wishes of the individual life when beset by one or another obstruction of Nature, at one or another time or place, they are accidental judgements. They do not concern life as a whole; they are not religious judgements.

When, however, judgements are necessary, in that they stand in inseparable connection with the person's conviction of the continuity of his own individual existence, they are religious judgements. All judgements which are thus grounded immediately in the inner experience of the person are religious. These experiences, and the judgements of which these experiences consist, are a part of his personal existence, which he cannot give up without destroying himself. Consequently beliefs of this kind are the expression of a practical necessity which under no circumstances the person can evade.

Another distinction between judgements of value would be the distinction between individual judgements, collective judgements, and universal judgements. A judgement which concerns one person only, which could not concern another person, cannot be religious. As soon as a man begins in the least to reflect upon the value of his own actions, he forms such judgements upon himself in countless numbers. Thousands upon thousands of these judgements of value upon self make a man what he is to-day. Extending over years they determine in one direction the general course of his life, determine his present choices, determine what he will be in years to come and what he will succeed in shaking off and dropping out of his character. Upon the basis of these judgements which he is constantly making, an intricate structure of purposes and values is building itself up within him. And in general, however much some of our choices seem childish, however much our inheritance and resources may differ, however much our outlook on life may be unequal, this structure within us of our own individual judgements invests each with a peculiar interest and with a certain human dignity.

Some kind of personal disposition, then, is formed in each man out of the mass of momentary judgements; and furthermore many individuals may coincide in their judgements. My values may be your values; my beliefs may be your beliefs. The interests of my family, of my friends, of my profession or of my nation are extensive interests common to many persons. Collective judgements are passed by all the members of such social units; these judgements express the collective value of an object for persons bound together by a common purpose. In proportion as the number of common interests increases and the feeling of community of purpose becomes more intense, these collective judgements acquire a different kind of validity. When the collective judgements reach the point that the individual would choose not to exist rather than violate them, they become religious judgements. All the multitudes of momentary choices become adjusted to a commanding social ideal. The single man despairs of himself, in case he be hindered from aiming at the social ideal, in case there is not any of his life that he can give to family, to blood-brotherhood or to city. His god expresses for him the value, in its might and majesty, of the ancestral life. His own life is a part only of one common life; it is the life of the others; and it is their life which is his life. His values are theirs; his best is what the common life chooses for him. That choice is, for him, his own value to himself. His life is inseparable from their judgement. Thus only his personality, as a whole, faces the world.

This common feeling of interest may cover humanity as a whole; the collective judgement becomes universal. If all men feel an interest in controlling Nature, the discovery of the stone-axe or of the Parthenon is of universal value. But it is evident that when I make such a judgement as universal and assert it as of value to all, I do not mean that by collecting evidence I have discovered in actual existence a universal common interest and a corresponding judgement; rather, I refer to a condition which ought to prevail among men. So long as I refer to an actual condition, it does not appear that the invention of the stone-axe or of the most recent machine is universally valued. But my appeal is not to one or another temporary or local consciousness, but to a consciousness which, as I maintain in this case, should prevail: this I call a normative consciousness.

Unconditionally we can assert a universal value when we know the extent of the class to which the particular objects should be of value: rifles to the soldier; beauty to the artist. Honour, friendship, health, insight, are now of absolute value in actual experience to all men whatsoever. Apparently, then, these judgements are universally valid, even though there be no actual relation between the object and my will, or rather, even though there be no other relation than that required for the repetition in ourselves of the judgement of the others.

Universal judgements, especially if they be religious, lose in vividness of personal feeling what they gain in extent of validity. Too easily they become regulative principles to which we assent in an impersonal tone of mind. They appear remote from ourselves and poor in quality when contrasted with sudden rushes of emotion which sweep us along for brief spaces with conviction and irresistible power.

We can agree that universal judgements are valid, and yet they appear rather pallid abstractions. We feel gaps when we must interpolate our judgements into the judgements of men distant in time and space and action. One living exception seems to neutralize all their validity. A homeless ascetic, striving day and night to deaden the clamour of appetite, could not easily assert the universal value of health. Health is to him the enemy of life. The breaking-down of health is his release from pain. Some of us, even here, may not count bodily vigour as an object of interest; some of us feel intensely the charm of the ascetic ideal. And yet as we interpret such a case the upshot would be, on the whole, a reassertion of the universal value of health. After the temporary doubt we wax bolder; we become even more certain that all men ought to desire health and set their wills upon it and find in it the keenest joy. Our final judgement is not much affected by a slight flaw in our inductions; it may even be contrary to them; for the judgement rests, first of all, upon the personal will, and then upon our imaginative subtlety in interpreting other wills. In more technical language we may assert our judgement as normative; we may assert that contrary judgements are abnormal; we appeal to an absolute normative consciousness, freed from our temporary and personal defects, to approve and to establish our assertion. Judgements such as these, without which the highest personalities cannot exist, are characteristic of the mystics and of the world-religions.

A religion consists in a personal feeling of the correspondence of one's self as a whole with some collective system of values; and, in more developed religions, with a normative system of values in addition to the collective system of values. A man who is religious in the fullest sense cannot live, unless he live upon the three levels at the same time, and unless he feel at one time the correspondences of the three levels within himself.

Many religions fail to reach the sense of correspondence with any normative system of values. Many religions also submerge vivid personal feelings under collective judgements of the clan, or of the caste, or of the city. The sense of one level may be defective, the sense of the other may be extremely faint. In the lower ancestral religions the individual's personal sense languishes; personal enthusiasms droop under the burden of usages. Glimmers of genius are carefully suppressed. Such religions may seem romantic to us to-day; but they seem romantic because mysterious, and because their troubles are remote from us and from our present troubles. Dreary enough they were to the few rare souls among them who asked for more life, for more of a sense of correspondence to something higher than such systems could generate. In the excessive collective systems of values of the Confucian or of the Roman ancestral religion, what we miss is a background of personal beliefs firm enough to break up some of the conventional mental habits of the clan. We miss the passions, focal enough and personal enough to discover and to create fresh values, hitherto unassimilated by the communal life.

The ability to discover higher correspondences within himself enables a man to have value for others. The lack of this ability is what we miss most in a friend. What we ask is not so much that he conform to usages of society, or that he sharpen his thinking powers, but rather that he express to us his best wishes and choices, his keenest enthusiasms and aversions. Then we can better estimate him as a man. Then we can find permanent common ground with the man himself. A change in this system of his feelings and impulses and likes is a readjustment of his personality. We wish this system to be firm, decisive and limitless in a man. In many of the ancestral religions, this system of personal feelings comes under the subjection of a power too strong for itself; for the individual is not strong enough to conceive the collective judgements of his clan to be a whole of which he is an active part; he conceives the collective judgements to be a rival will mightier always than himself. To him his life is inconceivable if independent of his clan; since his clan requires that he recognize the duty of entire conformity. No individual can progress unless he repeat the will of the clan; and repudiation of the established order severs the life of the man from his people.

But if he is sure enough of himself to appeal to a will more inclusive than the common will of any clan, he approaches the higher religions. He need not abjure and defy his clan. He asserts that his judgement is right. He means not only that this or that collection of persons actually so judges, but also that all ought so to judge. His demand would be brutal, if all he means is that others must adjust themselves to him. But his demand obtains its authority as soon as it appears that his new insight is guided by an ideal which any man can recognize within himself as authoritative over each of us. And so, in general, as well as in each one of us, we can discover deeper meanings which underlie any collective judgements. In every human life there slumbers a limitless will, an individuality, which each man is to develop not for the sake of himself, nor even for others, but which is to be recognized as having absolute value in itself. On our highest level our judgements are right, without regard to any one momentary value, without regard to the weight of collective judgements, without regard to pleasure or pain, without regard to single facts or feelings which express particular conditions or desires. A judgement of this kind is an expression of the activity of the person as a whole. This whole is felt to be in correspondence with one infinite system of beliefs which expresses one whole inclusive system of normative values, a will which unifies the purposes of human life.

In any one action we never succeed in expressing our

whole personality. No systems of verbal language or of symbolic actions are felt to be expressions of our complete self. The face of nature may be set against us; the face of society may know us not; we may feel helpless and despondent. But whatever we should count as the full expression of personal life, the life we desire, the life of self as one whole, that we should confess as our religion. Our religion is the larger life we feel within us, a part of ourselves, struggling with ourselves, the perfection of ourselves, to which we may always turn with passionate interest. This larger self, seemingly within us yet ever just beyond our reach, this it is that men have tried to represent in their conceptions of their gods. In our own experience we have the assurance of this life, at which we aim, and to which we incessantly return. This life cannot be altogether different from our own life, for it is that by which we measure our lives, that from which we cannot sever our lives, unless we ourselves cease to be. To this life we appeal whenever we assert a judgement, believing with all the intensity of our best selves that our judgement must be so; we appeal then from our transitory self, from social standards to an inclusive infinite will, never identical with any one of its moments, to a will which we trust will prevail, a will upon which we stake the best in our lives. In proportion as our normative judgements extend themselves within us, just so far they express in our own selves what this will must be. But since within us this will is confused with individual and collective values, the sense of what it means is broken and easily lost. The Absolute Will in us is the standard at which we aim and in which we hope for peace. It is beyond us because we will it more often than we know we will it. It is beyond us because we are really willing it, just when we are only aware of willing what is after all some temporary and provisional choice. In proportion, then, as we decide to take ourselves more seriously, we find that our life extends beyond any momentary boundary and is continuous with a region of life which we can never at any one time call our own. How far beyond us this region extends, we cannot say. But each single judgement that has ever actuated us, and all the values in the wills of others, in past and future, to which we have reacted, contribute to this wider region of our self. Each transitory act of will merges in this wider self, and passes completely beyond our control. Of this wider self our present condition is a constantly fluctuating expression. Various judgements have fallen into ordered series; other judgements have neutralized themselves in reciprocal conflicts. Each new value finds a correspondent in some inclusive series and each modifies the wider self. Each value exercises authority, minimal though it may be, and each uses its influence, imperceptible though this influence may appear to the actual self. This infinite self subsists by these unnumbered millions of self-subordinating values. The more stable groups, the collective groups, and above all the normative groups, gradually crystallize into reliable human wills and fixed institutions. Each part is in relation to the whole. But it is no less true that the whole inclusive will requires each part of itself,—each passion for order, and ungrudging friendship, and each appreciation of beauty, and loyal deed. Of these the Absolute Self consists. I stumble into an adventure, and I find that my wider self has brought me there. My whole self is facing the situation and interpreting the moment and weighing the mood. In such wise each distinguishable single value and the resultant choice of my total self must affect each other. Each value is found to be an expression of the wider self. And the Absolute Will is what it is in part, because of that particular choice.

Different natures and different wills develop in different ways. For some it seems more natural always to regard life as a whole; for others to take it as a collection of groups. Some develop harmoniously, others in detail and in variable and more one-sided ways. It is easier for some to find one ruling purpose and to focus their wills upon that; for others it is easier to adjust themselves frequently to examples of life or to different social ideals. In all cases, what we want is the inclusive system of purposes and the sense of correspondence to it. That is our religion. In this search we find our life and our encouragement; we find larger views of things opened to us; we discover that our life lies on higher levels than those which we have been too exclusively cultivating.

In the three following lectures we will consider (iii) a case of primitive beliefs as an illustration of individual judgements not yet in the strict sense religious; (iv) certain ancestral systems constructed by religious judgements of the collective class; (v) various mystical ideals which strive to exclude all judgements that are not normative.

LECTURE THIRD

III
PRIMITIVE BELIEFS

ANY expression of religion is an act of practical life. Its design is to make remoter values vivid to the present will, to adjust that will to the more difficult judgements upon life. Science of Religion displays to us the situations which call forth religious acts, the problems which require solution, the correspondences between different levels of life. It shows us first the easier religious solutions in the form of unquestioning following of usage, in the form of a kind of herd-instinct. Next, it shows us the veneration paid to men of force as objects of worship, as powers mysterious beyond all calculation, beyond all approach. Science of Religion shows us how much the clan-feeling can sustain the more remote aspirations and beliefs. It shows us also how the development of a strong tribal life may form the basis for the subtler feelings and shades of choice which prepare for the mystical religions. And it shows us finally that as the individual becomes more of an ordered whole, social control and social suggestion fail to assure him of the ultimate ends of belief. Your tribesman may continue the ceremonies: he may observe food restrictions, he may keep feasts, he may marry, he may give divine names to his children, he may initiate his youth, he may pay his respects to the mighty spirits with whom he has to do; but his beliefs have become more complex, and his requirements of action more varied, than the religion of his tribe can satisfy. The ancient order of beliefs is questioned; the older purposes are attained in new ways; the problems of life become more pressing and the emotions more sensitive. The ancient usages, the first attempts of the early clan, achieved much, accomplished what nothing else at the time could have accomplished so well. But now they do not seem so decisive: purposes are now more closely adjusted to new systems of beliefs; desires are fulfilled in other systems of voluntary control. There are new expressions of actual values. And all these are again personal acts of choice.

Science of Religion tries to discover these shifting systems of beliefs and scales of value. If the scientific descriptions of these religions are to interest us at all, if we say we understand the personal attitudes, we mean that we have put ourselves to some degree in the situation of the clansman. Our will is then his will; his belief might cause us to act as he acts. In that sense we understand his system of beliefs. We fit his, as a part, into our own scale of beliefs. We fit his beliefs into ours in terms of action and of personal choice, not in terms of fact or in verbal values. The experience is determined by the will, and the outer facts group themselves about it. The will being the object of search, the only way to find it is to let it affect us. However slightly, the poise of our will must change. We understand the strange creature whose will is laid bare before us in so far as we ourselves change. To that extent he becomes a part of ourselves. Thus there can be no science unless there be practice; if divorced, neither exists. My character influences my science; my science makes me other than I have been before. The relation is reciprocal. We may not heed the little shift in the balance of will; we may not know why our delight is a shade more keen, or our repulsion a shade less dull; but nevertheless our total system of beliefs has lost and regained a central point in order to include one more act of will. The higher the religion, the more these alterations of the whole self are expressions of a character forcible and well ordered on all its levels, able to predict and to verify its oscillations of centre with increasing success.

What, then, is the material to which the Science of Religion attempts to give this form? It is, first of all, a mass of ethnological work: descriptions of ideas, especially conceptions of gods; descriptions of rites; descriptions of customs under religious control; descriptions of arts expressing moods which accompany these ideas or actions. We are no longer content with sketches of religion from the tourist or the adventurer whose point of contact is momentary, who severs religion from ordinary life. There are now trained ethnologists, men with orderly minds, who quietly devote themselves to a people, as a skilful tutor lavishes life upon a boy. The assumption of the ethnologist is that the minds of uncultured men are not loose heaps of feelings and perceptions, but are as coherent systems as his own mind. All that is necessary is to find his permanent personal interests and the stimulations which make him feel most alive to himself; to discover what permanent ambition and goal of desire returns most frequently to his imagination; then we have found the man himself.

The brilliant work in Ceylon of two German naturalists, the brothers Sarrassin, gives us a description of one of the simplest attempts to express in an action a permanent object of desire. The Rock-Veddahs are one of the five or six most primitive peoples alive today. They have no agriculture; food is eaten without the use of fire. Their greatest skill is in the use of a ten-foot bow. The man lies on his back and holds the bow with his feet. He sinks his shafts up to the feather in the water-buffalo and sends them clean through the wild pig. All his interests, his satisfactions and triumphs are associated with this weapon. In the crises of his life, when there is sickness or childbirth or preparation for the hunt, there is worship of the arrow. In the forest at night the men dance in a circle around the arrow stuck tip down in the ground. There are fires to add to the festive character of the scene. There are rhythmic cries, expressions of thanks or of hope. This continues until all are worked up to almost convulsive excitement. But there is no clear concept of an arrow-spirit, or of a god, or of any soul. The dance expresses what they want; but the ideal is not so clear that it can be expressed in a concept or in a word or in a figure.

The emotions expressed in the dance and in the rude

cadences are pre-religious and pre-animistic rather than religious. The motions and sounds are the first crude efforts to express what might develop into a religion. They are dramatic symbols of the qualities which the Veddah values as the highest he can possibly conceive. They express himself when he seems most genuinely alive; they make him feel triumphant over himself and his hindrances.

But it does not appear that the series of beliefs in himself is sufficiently continuous to find expression in the conception of a spirit as a constantly active personal force, always alert, always master of the decisive stroke. The reason seems clear: the long foot-bow is too large a part of the whole effort. The weapon is too much for the man. The game is the victim of the arrow, not of the bowman. Furthermore, the game is shot while the man is at rest. No game is tracked through the maze of bamboos. The hunter does not trample through the jungle with all his senses intent upon the game. There is no pursuit; there is little variety of movement. What the forest sends he will shoot. Hence the plot is too brief. The emotions are intense, but spasmodic and unbalanced. The values within are not enough ordered to become projected outward as a compact and self-existent whole. The feelings are immersed in a half-conscious neutral flux. The beliefs do not form systems, nor can they crystallize into the conception of a god, corresponding to a man's life, but able to meet triumphantly the situations which baffle the man. Hence the Veddah cannot express his total self; and because he cannot express himself, his fellow-tribesmen cannot understand him or offer to sustain him when he tries to contrast himself with his world.

All this is ethnological. If we choose simple cases like this with few balanced masses of feelings, the mere imagination of the scene arouses sympathetic impulses in ourselves. The trunks of the great trees, the heavy swaying leaves, the flecks of sunlight through the branches, the birds and drowsy beetles, the insipid fragrances, all these sensations are keen in us. We can feel the suspense, the release of the shaft, the fall of the quarry, and the elation of the midnight festival. We feel traces of the impulses in ourselves. All that this imaginary experience of ours lacks in comparison with the actual experience of the bowman is the conviction of the reality of what we see and hear in imagination. The mass of our sensations may be the same in quality, but they lack the setting of his. Our world does not fit to his world. The scene causes us to act appropriately, but it commits us to no course of action. It cannot give us the delightful flavour of full reality. Yet in imagination we feast upon the details. The images group together; we face towards them, or we turn away. We have measured wills with the strange creature whose beliefs seem so distant from our own. Similarly, any simple passionate expression by another of sadness or of hope, betrays to us, within ourselves, latent tendencies to action far below the thin crust of sensation upon which our present life revolves.

If, however, the material is more complex, a deliberate effort to sympathize will be required. If the documents are not human but written, not only the material but the beliefs which interest us in the documents will vary in quality. The acts of will are no longer direct adjustments to momentary impulse. Beliefs which find expression in verse or in writing are already partly detached from the intense physical excitements which alone give the Veddah his chance to express his purposes. The minds of the men who make songs are of a paler and less resonant fibre. Sudden upheavals of the emotional apparatus are more rare. Fewer stimulations result directly in deeds. There are more interests which involve a long series of approaches to an end. If the feelings seem less vivid to us, it is because they are less physiological, and more evenly distributed. To the singer they seem more vivid; they are more the expression of his personality and less of his body. But all this, unfortunately, hides the beliefs in the song from him who is searching from without for the inner value of the song to the singer. To the observer from without the song expresses the person less candidly than the dance. The poet, the maker of the verse, cannot put himself into his words as pre-animistic man can throw himself without reserve into a lumbering bodily rhythm. The poet cannot easily lose himself in undirected passion; cannot give as much of himself with his song; nor can he use massive physical vibrations. He severs himself from his body; he faces his own body. The complexity of his beliefs prevents him from expressing himself completely. Consequently we do not find more of him in the poem than he has himself put there. When the song becomes prose it is still more depersonalized. It restrains beliefs and becomes a mere thread of abstractions and of hard outlines; it can speak only of what is common property; thus beliefs are spun out into generalities.

But in the Science of Religion we cannot accept anything verbal as having in itself personal value. Nothing impersonal, nothing abstract, can pass for religion. Words at their best are a kind of debased currency. Easily we forget how subsidiary a word is to the meaning which the user of the word gives it. Suppose now we have a great mass of incantations, epitaphs, rituals, meditations, books of origins, formulas of salutations, and dreams of the life of the soul. How can these words have value to us? How can we arouse in ourselves sympathetic reactions? Can we, in any degree, repeat the quick judgements and the emotions of the man who used these very words when beset by starvation or death, or by brutal tyrants? Or can we repeat the feelings of the victor exulting in harvests, and bright skies, and in deliverance from enemies?

The belief of the man who used the words can be a value to us only so far as we can compare the imagined inner mental states of the stranger with our own inner life. Otherwise we may translate the hymn, we may edit the manuscript, and publish as many texts as we please, but we shall remain dead to the religion expressed in the words. Any religion that we can understand must be a sense of correspondence of values which are alive within us. We must reconstruct the inner meaning out of beliefs of our own. We must imagine ourselves feeling the values as the harvester or the bacchanal or the anchorite felt them. Then our feelings fall directly into some kind of a unified belief. There will be new impulses to act, a new balance, and a new act of will crystallizing about the verbal picture. If we have any heart for sorrow of our own, if we can feel delight ourselves, then we can interpolate feelings of our own into the record. But it is of ourselves that we vitalize the words. Constantly we test the attitude which we have developed artificially within ourselves; from this process we acquire a keener sense of the difference between our ordinary state of mind and that which we are trying to reproduce. As the distinctions become more clear, as we decide how we ourselves should act if we were equipped with the stranger's sensations, we begin to estimate the value to ourselves of the religion which we are trying hypothetically to feel. And in proportion as our own religion implies much to ourselves, the nearer our reconstruction will be to the other's actual belief. In the experiment our own judgement will become much more definite to ourselves, and the belief of the other will seem real as never before. A sharp contrast of will gives us a firmer poise and gives the stranger the freshness of life.

This reconstruction of another's will is a familiar process to us. Every drama we have read is an experiment of this kind. Delight in the drama is distinct from the mere reading of the pages. Our aesthetic pleasure and our artistic judgement demand far more than accurate reading. If the characters of the drama are to be more than names, we must feel their passions, their ecstasies and their pains; we must feel their suspense. But the feelings and beliefs which make the characters must be in us. To some of us Lear is a mere name; the words he speaks are sounds with no values. To others he is a person more distinct than we are ourselves. To some of us Maeterlinck's Mélisande is a wan and repellent caricature, to others a definite and impressive character. In other words, we might say that Lear and Antigone are merely words, not persons, until we make them alive out of our own store of human passions. It is not that we imitate feelings alien to ourselves, but rather, out of the dim background of feeling in ourselves we bring forth a grouping, uncombined hitherto, of our own feelings, now first unified by the genius of the dramatist, henceforth permanent in us under the name Antigone or Lear. These characters, then, are objectifications of feelings. It is our own feelings which we see pass before us as Lear or as some ethereal creature with an Attic or a Gallic name; they are definite objects; they live within us a life of their own.

Quite distinct is another kind of feeling. We take sides with or against the persons of the drama; we avoid them or welcome them; we reject them or accept them; our sympathy goes to them or we hold aloof; we suffer with their agony. These feelings are not those which constitute the persons of the drama; these feelings are not objects to us; they are sympathetic feelings; they are our personal attitudes towards the characters already formed; they are the reaction of the observer to the object of his attention.

At the end of the drama there are, besides these sympathetic feelings, yet other personal feelings.

There is a resultant mood; we are exultant in spite of the sight of falseness and of pain, in spite of our own doubt and gloom. The feeling towards the drama as a whole results in a new total feeling of our own. The total self includes now a new insight into life; it has felt itself in new activities. A judgement has found total expression, complete in itself, in a work of art which for the moment has seemed the world. The little world of this drama has its own stubbornness and its own savagery; it has also delicate and beautiful and reckless devotions. Both of these aspects of this drama must now find their place in my inner world. Both have affected myself. Both result in a new relation of myself to the world.

Thus the drama may bring us back to religion in that it makes clearer how religious conceptions of the gods might be formed. In some similar way, we must lend life out of ourselves if we are to understand the meaning of a tribal god, or of the great Indra, or of Dionysus. We bring a mass of concrete, often very trivial, tales into consciousness. We empty our own minds of our usual reflections, and by a slight strain of attention we make the descriptions of the gods alive with our own personal prejudices and passions.

Directly, then, the god is alive, as alive as Hamlet, alive with beliefs of his worshippers. So the concept of the god also consists of objectified feelings; he expresses how the world should be to win human love and approval. In a symbol the concept of the god expresses a standard of worth by which the world is to be judged. Similarly, the sympathetic feelings towards the persons in the drama would correspond to the human loyalties to the god as king or as moral leader. Such sympathetic loyalties give new structure to the stuff of which life is made; and they express a kind of belief which we hope will be a part of the total expression of our lives. And finally, the resultant feeling, as the drama ends, would correspond to the deep religious belief that through the world one vast purpose runs, one life, one plan which we have followed, which for a time we have understood,—one plan which we accept as the complete fulfilment of all our beliefs, a plan to which all that is best in us is now felt to correspond.

LECTURE FOURTH

IV

ANCESTRAL SYSTEMS

THE advance from the prehuman ancestor to man is said to be marked by three discoveries: the use of fire, the use of weapons, and the use of words as a supplement to gesture language. To make good use of these inventions man needed yet another discovery of another kind. He needed to discover that a man's life is worse off and not better if he continues to assume that human life is so small an affair that its outcome is a matter of indifference. That assumption cannot be of much practical value. It leads men easily to a kind of placid despair, to the feeling that effort is futile. Wherein lies the root of this indolent assumption? Clearly, it is in the assumption that the individual human being is self-sufficient; that he need recognize no obligations nor do anything for reasons, unless he choose; or that he need not even find reasons for what he wants to do. The discovery required was religion, the discovery that each man can accept as the fulfilment of his own purpose a purpose made actual in a society, and at the same time rooted in reality. This discovery of the correspondence of one's own purpose with the purposes of society gave a meaning and a value to life which the blind obedience to animal impulses had not given. So long as man knew nothing more than the healthy action of his own body, and so long as his chief delight was in plenty of unimpeded massive sensations,—such as self-abandonment to the crude rhythms of his dance,—his experience would be too simple to require a religious reaction. But as his organism becomes finer, his experience wider, and the demands for action more varied, the joy in purely physical action and in massive emotional upheavals is less frequent. Many ends, as he finds, cannot be attained in isolated bursts of passion; many ends can be attained only when he is conscious of acting by choice as a member of a group, or as a part of a whole. Social loyalties will add to his own valuation of himself; because they give him the confidence he needs to face the purposeless forces of the world. Religion is a device which helps him to attain this goal, that is, to find himself expressed in his loyalties and to discover the worth of this correspondence by testing its structure in the stuff of his own experience. Religion is also a device to overcome situations of social tension, which, as he has found, make his life as a self-sufficient individual impossible. At the same time it is a device to control the actions of the tribe. Certain common habits are found to correspond; certain purely individual habits are rejected. The man finds his self in his social habits and loyalties. He finds himself organized with over-individual aims in view, with aims, that is, which extend beyond the range of his individual life. The maintenance of the social body begins to have a supreme value in itself; and it assures to the individual the preservation of the ends without which he cannot live. It is surely true that extreme situations of emotional tension result, in almost every case, in the formation of new conceptions. The end which releases him from such tensions, if it be an end upon which he will stake his life, is represented in an idea of a god. The god is the picture of the man released from imperfections and tensions, unbalked by body, or beasts, or cosmic weather. The god is the concept embodying some latent perfection restricted within the man. If this idea of the god be accepted by the group as its social ideal, the first step in religion is taken. The idea of a tribal god expresses collective judgements which are religious. As soon as the concept of the god no longer oscillates with the individual's moods, it attains a fixed character. It expresses a collective value; it expresses more than an emotion emerging and diffusing in one man; it asserts a definite solution, by a body of persons, of certain problems of life. When the assertion is firm, if the men are daring and persistent, they see the fulfilment of their purpose, they behold the god doing with ease the deeds they have never done in this world. Henceforth common actions are controlled by a comparison with the god's completed act. The concept grows more definite as it represents more life, as it includes more beliefs, as it orders more values, as it gives more direction to the actions of the group. The god assumes authority over all who feel the need of correspondence between their own lives and the ideal action which he symbolizes. The god begins to feel the unwavering support of the tribal will. He becomes independent of any single experience. He enters into a close communion with each member of the common life. His life is inseparable from their life; their life is worthless if severed from his life. Their social rites and usages are exercises in imitation of his life. Their hymns urge them on to feel the joy of completed effort as he feels it; to feel the world, in actual experience, as a responsive whole, wherein false notes and discords persistent in man are resolved into one harmony including the single tones.

An example of the formation of the idea of a personal protector, and of the expansion of this concept into the concept of a god expressive of the collective beliefs of a society, is given us in an accurate and very subtle study of the religion of the Omaha tribe. In the Legend of the Sacred-Pole, Miss Fletcher tells us how the Sioux boy obtains his protector. The legend recounts how this protector was first discovered. "The people felt themselves weak and poor. The old men gathered together and said, 'Let us make our children cry to Wakonda.' So they took their children, covered their faces with soft clay, and sent them forth to lonely places. The old men said, 'You shall go forth and cry to Wakonda. When on the hills you shall not ask for any particular thing. Whatever is good that may Wakonda give.'" This rite has been observed up to the present day. The boy is told what he is to do, moistened earth is put upon his head and face, a small bow and arrows are given him. He seeks a secluded spot on some high hill; and under the pines he chants the prayer; he lifts to heaven his hands wet with tears and then lays them on the earth; he fasts, until at last after some days he falls into a sleep or trance. If in his dream or trance he hear or see anything, that thing is to become the special mediator through which he receives aid. Then, the ordeal over, the youth returns for food and rest. No one questions him, but at the end of four days he confides his vision to some old man, and starts out to find the animal he has seen in his trance. The totem is the symbol of this animal. The totem is the most sacred thing he can possess. By it his natural powers are to be reenforced so as to give him success as a hunter, victory as a warrior, and even ability to see into the future.

The assumption in this belief is that all things animate and inanimate are pervaded by one common life, called *wakonda* or *orenda*. This life is continuous and cannot be broken.

The men who have received the same vision group together. This is the simplest form of social action. Those who see the bear make up the Bear Society; those to whom the thunder comes form the Thunder Society. The tribe is formed by certain fixed relations between these totem-bands, and all these totem-bands receive their organization from the *wakonda.*

The concept of the god is then a statement by the tribe of its collective values for life. It matters little how logical the concept be, provided social values are embodied in it, and provided the actions of the individual and the impulses of the tribe are governed and lifted up towards this concept. It matters much that the concept should embody in vivid form conduct of life indispensable to the tribe as a whole.

If now we should wish to repeat or to understand in any degree the beliefs and loyalties burning in the soul of the youthful initiate, we must strip off, for a moment, layer after layer of mental categories with which, so far as we are civilized, we have overladen the passions of the primitive man within ourselves. This is not such a difficult process for us to-day. When we see the paroxysms of our young men supporting with their voices the efforts of their comrades in the games, we are in range with similar mental levels. In the minds of youth intent upon such contests there are no obstacles to prevent the will from focusing upon a single scale of values. The objects of consciousness are unclassified except with reference to the desire to surpass the opponent. If these objects of consciousness could find themselves expressed in the concept of a single animal which should express in actions the harsher predatory passions surging to and fro from margin to margin of consciousness, we should be very near the attitude of will in the Sioux boy. A certain course of action is extremely prized. By training his mind and body for days, the Sioux boy expels from his mind concepts discordant with this course of action. He fills his mind with pictures of heroes; these heroes are the animals; and their deeds are examples of life. He regards these animal heroes with sincere admiration. His life is spent in contention with them. When he is alone, they surpass him in power. The more he thinks of them the more his life is effective, the more valuable he becomes to his tribe. If he is untrue to the ideal of life expressed in the animal, his life is left without guidance. We civilized men cannot so easily express supreme aims in life by symbols which are living animals. And furthermore, those who direct our education do not encourage us so to express ourselves, or teach us to boast of ancestry from a wolf or from a raven. But if we could for a moment imagine ourselves subjected to similar influences, I think we may assume that our imagination might take the same course. It is only that our training has been for fifty generations in a very different direction. Our education aims to reduce the force of any one such emotion. We strive to make it impossible for a man to reduce himself to a single scale of values until he become an inert mass so far as other values are concerned. If one of us should so reduce himself, we should say that such a one does not know what he is about, although the individual in question might assure us he feels very much alive. To-day above all other habits of mind we encourage reflection. In types of mind like the Sioux, men living in compact groups bound together by blood relationships, there is almost no reflection, or at least no habit of reflection. Even in advanced cases of the same type, in the ordinary life of the Greek city or of the Roman gens, there was the same lack of reflection, the same inability to feel more than one scale of values at a time, and the same passive mind overwhelmed by the weight of collective beliefs. There were no habits of experiment or of discussion, and but little analysis of objects. There was no questioning of the value of sensations. There was no search for the origin of an idea or for its right to existence. Every idea was accepted without reserve and as it appeared. The apparent and the real were identical. It would appear, then, that we can never think as the Sioux thinks, or as men in the fields of Attica thought. Still after all, since man has existed, the world, in its main outlines and in its laws, has not changed. The nervous mechanism and the simple sensations seem much the same. It is the grouping of sensations that has changed. The composition, the structure, the methods of classifying the mental units, have greatly changed. Thus it might yet be possible to dissever the primitive layer from the derived layers of consciousness, the simple from the complex.

Consequently if we wish to repeat the scale of values or the system of beliefs of the Omaha Indian, or of any other ancestral system, or of any belief in one common soul life reincorporating itself in the transitory lives of individual members of the tribe, we must strip ourselves of our modern habits of mind,—we must simplify the classification of our sensations aud cultivate a less active mind.

This means that all modern philosophy, which invariably has taught that the human understanding has an activity and an individuality of its own, must be given up. Aristotle also, who taught that each single act considered in itself is our work, although as a whole the active intellect is a portion of the divine reason, must be abandoned. Plato was convinced that a man contributes nothing to the elaboration of any active states; he does not even suspect the presence in himself of a power to change his thoughts. To Plato's thinking, ideas come from without, intermingled, easy to confound; yet each is complete in itself. There are no degrees in the assimilation of impressions. Ideas are poured into us as water into a pool. The soul contributes nothing to the existence, or to the grouping, or to the changes of sensations.

One step backward beyond Plato brings us into another mental world. We are on a level with the clansmen of the Iliad, we are mental contemporaries of the Buddha, we are not far from the world of the Omaha. If we can find our way at all in this world, we find it is arranged in very simple mental series. There, one must search to find any general ideas, or more than a few abstract terms. But there is a sea of crude feeling, of antipathies and loyalties. The individual can feel only a single strong emotion at one time. All other feelings than the one strong emotion are felt only in common with a mass of men. Insight is shallow, and self-possession is easily relaxed. Each man is an automatic mass of blind impulses, a mass which passively collects social stimulations. Like a physical contagion, courage comes from without. Cowardice, likewise, is something not ourselves. Now the gods are the names of the permanent and more mighty of these emotions. The god launches forth a passion and descends upon men as a stampede comes over a drove of cattle. All critical turns in life, the power of attack at the right instant, the unaccountable weakening in emergencies,—this is the work of gods, or is it not rather, the god himself? Passions, desires and judgements are, at best, tools, weapons or ornaments borrowed in times of unexpected stress. Passions and judgements do not belong to a man, do not arise in him, and are not part of himself. Passions rove about the world; they are sent into a man; they surge through the empty spaces within him; they sting the inert body into frenzy. These nomad inhabitants of the mind, to us pale subjective conflicts of values, are to him living things, active wills, realities more real than himself. Any unaccountable event, even the quiver of the leaf fluttering unexpectedly in the breeze, may be the action of some god. If strange passions become persistent in him; if they require his constant attention; if they become of such importance that the whole tribe is compelled to take an attitude towards them, then the god has proved the passion to be his act. In other words, the passion expresses such judgements upon life that life cannot continue indifferent to these judgements. Life is not a whole without them. The judgement is then a religious judgement. Society may fall to pieces if these judgements are ignored. Social institutions are held together by hospitality to the passions of the more majestic of these wandering gods. Each of the gods has his fixed programme of action. A man cannot live the night through if he has forfeited the respect of the gods for him or lost their love. He cannot be himself if estranged from them. If he be in sore distress, he cries out to the great over-lord, heretofore remote at the circumference of human living, but now swiftly approaching the centre of his life.

Great emotions and the release from great emotions both come, then, from without. The decisive stroke is usually the act of a god. The value of the act has nothing to do with the individual will. The relation between a man and his thoughts is almost the reverse of the normal relation as we think of it to-day. The man's mind is more like the mind of a child or of a hypnotized subject. The great passion lives; it energizes in the man; he is its docile tool, and is less alive than the passion in him. The man himself hesitates to act. It seems impossible to act; yet some deed must be done. Then it is that the god puts decision into the man.

If, now, the god be the conceptual embodiment of such a passive herd-instinct, the positive human gain of this system of beliefs becomes forthwith quite palpable. In the social life the interests of each individual depend upon the welfare of the whole group. Each life is forfeit to each other life. The original animal instincts, the sex instinct, the lust of the power to kill, the cry of hunger, the need of protection for property and self, might yield to the more human interests of admiration, of respect, of delight in common purposes, of disinterested affection. The more firm the texture of the tribal life, the greater would be the dependence of the individual, and the more insistent his wish that the customs of the clans be conserved.

Thus, in ancestral systems, the concept of the god which expresses the social ideal might widen until the god might be conceived as the guardian of the collective life of the clan. At the same time, social usages, the resultants of past and present individual purposes, would be the bonds by which the god would hold his tribe together. It may be the god is a deified ancestor; his quality in battle and in councils of the tribe is known. By effective living he has won his way to leadership; the tribe respects him and loves him for his work. His will expresses the tribal will. His will represents voluntary loyalties and voluntary restrictions of purely individual desires. The concept of the god would express a resultant ideal and is also an actual will. Some such expression of the resultant ideal is a necessary condition for the more complex social life of a clan. The god is then more than a temporary passion or even guardian; he becomes the undying king. He himself is offended in case his will be transgressed. The correspondence is complete;

each single will finds fulfilment in him, the symbol of the collective purpose of the tribe. Such a system implies a disinterested choice of social values; yet there is never an entire break with individual interests. Two great levels correspond: the god, the representative of the common ideals of the tribe, is conscious of a social dignity of his own; and again, each man, under the guidance of the god, secures his own personal welfare. In terms of ritual, the god delights in sacrifices, the physical signs of deferential affection towards himself, and, correspondingly, he rescues his worshippers who love him and obey him; or, conversely, he thwarts the impious who pay him no devotion or who lightly mutilate customs of which the life of his tribe consists. Thus, trust in the will of the god and the personal feeling of obligation correspond; and the will of the god embodies the sanction of right; personal moral ideals inhere in the will of the god; and his will is the moral imperative.

In such wise the half-brutal and egoistic intercourse between gods and men weakens on both sides; and common interests in conduct and in art, and a common sense of self-respect, are correspondingly stronger. The fulfilment of life is over-individual, the full value of life cannot be attained by a solitary will. The criterion of value cannot depend upon any one will; the criterion of right is the will to serve a social ideal such as to include and preserve the wider interests of each member. The god embodies the collective ideal; he rises above the bare impulses of animal life; at the same time selfish motives as reasons for worship become meaningless and offensive.

Some sense of correspondence of these two levels, (of the individual impulse and of the collective values,) is one of the features without which no religion can be complete.

The defect of the ancestral system would probably be that the god wavers, and knows not how to lead. It may be that the god has not learned to reflect as soundly as he knows how to act. If such a god be compelled to deliberate, he becomes less imposing. He has been wont to strike out first, and forecast his action after. Later this course suffices not for successful guidance of the tribe. If now it appear necessary to think before acting, such deliberation, to such a mind as his, might seem to be the feeling that he is the accidental meeting-point of two possible courses of action.

The ancestral god is the embodiment of the social ideal of action. If, then, he hesitates to act, he must abdicate. This means that the system of collective beliefs, if not supplemented by normative beliefs, now proves inefficient. This is the stage through which all Europe was passing when the Platonists and Christians were upheaving the consciences of men.

Normative beliefs or positive mystical beliefs prove most effective precisely at the point where the social ideal begins to break down, at the point where the great world-religions begin to add normative standards to merely collective ideals. And at this point human life begins to make for itself a new and a nobler world.

LECTURE FIFTH

V

MYSTICAL IDEALS

MYSTICISM always presupposes more or less highly elaborated social systems. Mystical ideals are most likely to supervene when the social ideal begins to waver. But, from the point of view of society, an ascetic mysticism, at its best, must be a temporary and restricted business. It intervenes, provisionally, after the old ideal can no longer dominate the clan. It may not be said under just what conditions mysticism begins to break through the social mind; but very often it dawns upon the mind when men begin to meditate upon the force of words; especially when the word is a concept of great dignity and when the stream of consciousness narrows and centres repeatedly upon that word.

Among the Iroquois Indians, when the chief of one of the two phratries dies, it is the duty of the one phratry to condole with the other for its loss. The phratry must install another person. It must give this person the title and the insignia of the dead chief. It must bring the dead chief to life in the person of his successor. All this is accomplished by the potency of a ritual. Unfortunately, the ritual does more: the words are so mighty that the ceremony cannot be held in the spring or in the summer. For then the words might kill the seed for planting, or blight the growing grain and fruits. It appears that the power exerted by the words is more than sufficient to promote the welfare of the tribe. If its use is untimely, it destroys the food of the tribe. This mystic power is the force in the word itself. The force of the word is conceived as physically as the body which expresses the force of the dance. The meaning of the word is a physical act. All the changes of inorganic matter are thought to be a kind of music chanted by physical things. The sounds produced by the life of the forest are expressions of the wills of animate beings. The trees and animals are exercising the mystic power of their rituals. Since all motions of bodies are thought to be acts of living beings, and since motions are accompanied by sounds, sounds are the evidence that some will is exerting a mystic potency with the intention of effecting some purpose. The cry of a bird, the sigh of the wind, the voices of the night, the moaning of the storm, the cracking of river-ice, are conceived to be the chants of various bodies giving forth words in the exercise of mystic power. Mr. Hewitt, who tells us of this, to whom the Iroquois is native speech, informs us that this power which the Iroquoians trust is called *orenda.* The same concept is found among other peoples. A few cases may suggest to us the force of this idea to the Iroquoian mind: if a youth, in a game of skill, overcomes another, his *orenda* overcomes the *orenda* of the other; if clan is pitted against clan, in public games, men reputed to possess powerful *orenda* are engaged to suppress the *orenda* of the antagonists; when a storm is brewing, the storm-maker is preparing *orenda.* Thus, singing means that the singer or chanter, whether he be beast, bird, wind, tree, stone or man, is putting forth his mystic power to execute his will. The medicine-man chants in imitation of one of the beings about him: it may be an insect or beetle, it may be the locust. The locust is called the Corn-Ripener. When it sings early in the morning, the day is hot and the corn will ripen. The inference is that the locust controls by his chant the summer heat and the crops of maize. His singing is the exertion of his *orenda* to bring on the heat necessary to ripen the corn. In like manner the rabbit sings, and by cutting the bark at the right height, indicates the depth of the winter's snow. The *orenda* controls the falling of the snow. Again, the word which is equivalent to the verb "to pray" does not signify a petition, but, rather, signifies an act which indicates that he who desires something from the body controlling an *orenda* must first lay his own *orenda* down. The sentence-word, "he prays," would then imply defeat, surrender, self-abnegation or a plea for life.

The Iroquois interprets the activities of the whole of nature to be a ceaseless struggle of one *orenda* against another. To obtain welfare he must exert his own *orenda* or employ devices, gifts, praise or self-abasement to persuade other more powerful beings to exert their *orenda* in his behalf. But gradually, in the stress of practical life, he unveils the weakness of the *orenda* in which he has learned to trust. He searches for more inclusive and more powerful charms. By means of obtaining favours and gifts from the more vigorous and insistent wills in the environment, he discovers the great collective *orenda*, that is, the gods. His religion is then a highly developed system of words and symbolic acts, in intricate complications, employed to control the Iroquoian world. Life consists in the ability to keep in touch with the mysterious chants which fill the world. Success consists in mastering the chants which really count. Mystic power is inherent in all things; it is everywhere, and over and below everything. There is nothing which is beyond it. All social usages become affected by it. It keeps unbroken the thread of life running through all things.

This idea of the *orenda* lacks only a certain aesthetic definiteness to engender one of the great mystical beliefs. A similar system of ideas, with regard to one power inherent in all things, prevails upon the peoples on the west African coast. The negro is more advanced in embodying his religious conceptions than the American Indian. His sense of rhythm is more sensitive. His feeling for the cosmic sequences is more acute. His lunar and solar myths are more complex. He has vague notions of time reading back into incalculable distance; he has a suspicion that there are fixed procedures for the whole of things. The great cosmic rhythms impress him in half-conscious fashion; but they do not rouse him to question them. He is aware of them only so far that he would be amazed if they should cease. These suspicions of cosmic regularity are associated in his mind with the distant spirit of the sky. The clear day-sky is not subject to change. His calm overarching vault is above all; he overshadows and includes all. No one can say when he came into existence. He is beyond the chances and changes of human life. Thus, the first glimmering sense of a permanent world-order is associated with a perceptible object. The experience of a permanent cosmic series embodies itself in the visible image of the heavens. But the unchanging spirit of the sky comes a little closer to human life in that he receives to himself the spirits of the dead. The souls of those whose bodies are clothed in night are led upward to the spirit of the sky. The air is filled with such souls; they are conducted to his beatific repose. Their lives then continue unchanged with him. Life itself, like the serene, outspread, all-protecting sky-spirit, is seen to be the everlasting, the only permanent fact. There is no such thing as destruction of life; there is no creation of life; there is no expectation of death.

This African system of beliefs, like the Iroquoian, just falls short of development into a clear mystical system. But in some respects the African is a little farther away than the American Indian, inasmuch as the symbol of the one eternal idea is drawn from the outer and visible world. The African system seeks its god in deserts of space and time, in outer immensities, in inferences built upon direct sensations. It cuts him off from human values. It prevents the stream of consciousness from internalizing itself upon a single concept of unsurpassable dignity.

If the African were mentally capable of regarding fixedly the conception which forms itself in his mind; if he could have felt it less sensuously and more as a concrete expression of his own inner life unified and harmonized in a single majestic concept; if he could have lived more consistently upon its level and refrained from sportive and repellent fancies with regard to it, it might suggest in some dim way the Indo-European Sky-Father and the Indo-European Fate, it might have led him close to the brink of a superb mystical faith such as we find in India or among the later Greeks.

The Greeks were worshippers of another sky-god. Their great Sky-Father was not content to remain in a beatific condition of perpetual drowsiness, which is the perfection of bliss to the mind of the indolent negro. Zeus was an active god. At times, however, he deliberated before acting. He selected not only a fixed end, but also a connected series of means to the end. But again, Zeus was uncertain how to choose; then to escape embarrassment, he weighed in his hand the balanced scale. To us this scale is the symbol of justice. To the old Ionians it was nothing of the kind. All it meant to them was that the Sky-Father in perplexity was attempting to avoid deliberate injustice. On his part it was less the symbol of justice than the sign of blind and brutal evasion of difficult action. The scale signified the need of an intervention of Fate, the Spoken Word. From without, Fate acted upon Zeus, in like manner as Zeus from without acted upon men. To the older thinkers Fate signified the resultant action of a sum total of forces which were unknown to the individual, not a mysterious voice, inaccessible, lowering upon the world, sending forth from an abyss irrevocable decrees. This may be the conception of Aeschylus, but it was not the old Ionian Fate. Fate connected itself in an especial form with the Sky-Father, who was in no sense infinite. Zeus had a beginning. He was not in all places. His knowledge was limited. His power was great, but the gods did not always obey him. He had no control over death. He could not restrict the action of an oath when it was once well launched.

An oath was a living reality, with wings, an armed divinity traversing the world, ready to rush upon men who forgot, upon men of bad faith, upon the gods.

This oath was the essence of the conception of Fate so far as the Sky-Father was concerned. He was limited most of all by his own *orenda*, as the Iroquois would say. Fate was the unified action of his own words and of all that passed beyond the actual personality of the god. But it does not seem to have been a distinct and isolated force. His Fate, the necessity which constrained, had its essence within himself. His Fate, the necessity which endured, was the after-effects of his own thinking. It is not a simple aspect of the nature of Zeus immanent in his substance. It was objectified, yet still not a personality complete in itself and eager to check him. It permeated all. It enfolded and directed all human and divine wills. It gave wretchedness or joy; it supplied steadiness of purpose; it enriched the sensuous life; it called forth decisions. It alone was always alert in the world in each event, in each change of form, in each idea and action. The Ionian Fate is an advance from the Iroquoian *orenda* and also from the west African sky-spirit. But to the Ionian it never seemed quite clear whether the Sky-Father and Fate were distinct or not. So long as beliefs associated with the visible sky or with any other cosmological symbol adhere to the concept of Fate, it must remain at the margin of consciousness; it cannot easily satisfy longings aroused within a man by experiences of his own inner life; it does not arise in his own heart as an immediate reality, and so it cannot give expression to a classical mysticism.

In India the development of mysticism was from the beginning uninterrupted, more recklessly logical, less repressed by social restraint. Here social life was stagnant; the individual intellect was intensely keen. Meditation upon the meanings of language has always been one of the most important occupations of the Indian mind. To us of European stock it seems that any one spoken word stands in two kinds of relations: one, the relation of the sound to the idea which it symbolizes; the other, the relation of the sound to the external meanings of words. To us, both of these relations seem artificial and conventional. Individual variations, changes in social habits and physiological details all affect the relations of word and idea and meaning to each other.

To the Indian mind the relation of these three was

much less loose. The word spoken, the vibration of air, was the immediate continuation of the idea, the auditory sensation, in the mind. Immediately the idea becomes a movement; immediately the idea becomes a meaning in relation with other words. To the Hindu these three, sound, idea and meaning, together form an indissoluble whole, a single indivisible reality. Of these three aspects the most conspicuous seems the most important. It appears to be the source of the other two. The spoken word gives the most vivid impression; it plays steadily its own rôle in the world; it strikes the ear; it holds the curiosity. Hence, it seems to have value to give to the other two aspects. To us it appears that the meaning creates the language: a man speaks, we should say, because he thinks. To the Hindu it seems less apparent that this is always the fact. Logically and temporally, the word seems to precede its idea and its meaning: a man thinks, the Hindu would say, because he is talking. The benefactor of the race would be, not a Prometheus who brings a few sparks from above, but he who releases among men the most finished of all forces, an irresistible word.

We think of words as receiving their meaning from

us. In themselves they are only intricately woven waves of air. But to the Indian, words exist in themselves, and have their values in themselves. They are alive. Like all living beings they have preferences and repulsions, aptitudes and passions. One word associates with another, and avoids a third. Each word is a force: it forms permanent combinations, or it destroys other words. Each sentence is a combination of forces. Every phrase exerts a positive material action, quite as perceptibly as air or as a storm of wind. Each has a fixed moral character. All of these energies belong to the word, as heat to the sun or as danger to night. Powerful words transform the life of the dead or create life. In the Rig-veda the adoration of the word reaches its highest point of splendour. Chants are directed to the word. The word passes on to new triumphs; it commands the gods; it regulates the totality of life; it keeps order in the three worlds. Even more it accomplishes: it not only governs, but is the source of order. It ends chaos, it begins the world.

By the help of the philologists, we can trace in India the growth of the mystical interpretation of life in the history of a single word. In the oldest mantras of the Veda, the word *brahman* has the very simple meaning of a charm or utterance of peculiar potency. As a house is built by carpenters, these words, as complete external wholes, are fashioned by the seers. But though external to man, and complete in themselves, they have yet an internal meaning. The world rests upon a *brahman; a brahman* is the truth; all things exist in it; the seven seers subsist upon it. The power internal in the structure of the *brahman* is at the heart of all things.

To the thinking of Eastern peoples this inner meaning, resident in the sum total of existence, is the one idea of unsurpassable dignity. The sole reality is a single all-embracing meaning. Within the Brahman every individual, everything concrete, is as if it were not. To-day at this day's dawn, as the sun's golden arms were raised aloft before his coming to enliven the world, every good Hindu, scholar or peasant, has prayed:

> *"That longed-for glory of the heavenly Savitar*
> *may we win,*
> *And may himself enlighten our prayers."*

This longed-for glory is the great Self, the all-embracing meaning in each one of us.

Thus, the Self of each of us can be stated in cosmological terms; and again, the unknown ground of all reality is identical, within the limits of its range, with ourselves. This does not mean that man is equivalent to Brahman. It does not mean that the highest reality we know must include the best in ourselves, and more, within itself. It means that this Brahman is the eternal unchanging reality within each of us, itself changeless amid all change. It is not external to any of us; it is not an unknowable something; but it is the only reality to which we have sure access. It is wider and more comprehensive than any present grouping or collection of our concepts or desires. In respect to Brahman we are absolutely unchangeable; in all other respects we are a ceaseless series of trivial fluctuations.

The same system of ideas, with some variation in expression, is set forth in the Yoga philosophy of Patanjali and in Buddhism. The narrower and shallower part of us, consisting of names and concepts and superficial conscious motives, is likened to an expanse of water. The seven changing forms of consciousness, the five sensations, the feeling of pleasure and pain, the feeling of self, are like waves on the water; water and waves are in hopeless disorder; each fluctuation is caught in conflicting rhythm. Each body lives in the same sense as each wave is a portion of the great expanse of water. As the wave is set in motion by movements of the atmosphere, so the fluctuations of our minds are driven onwards by ignorance. Each human life is a portion of the great over-soul. While the body lives, the over-soul is a person in bodily form; when the body is dead, that person exists no longer. Only the over-soul remains, of which the individual was a part, as the body of water remains when the waves cease to fluctuate. The over-soul is that unchanging will within us and without us, no longer, as it now seems to us, broken into fragments by the unceasing interruptions of ignorance. We cannot name it; it is all internal meaning; while every name is external; every name is an illusion. It is called unnamable that we may rid it of names. It is that of which our little minds can assert and deny nothing except that it is, and is one, and is self-complete.

Every one, then, may know himself directly and give his own self some kind of guidance. Every one may find his own self. The method is to transcend momentary consciousness by an effort of will. All concepts belong to that which changes; there must be something unchanging in dependence upon which all concepts exist. All representations are mixed with illusions. We must search for our permanent and original nature. We must train ourselves to repress representations of objects. There are different ways of training the mind. One way is to sit still, closing the eyes and keeping the mind as quiet as possible until self-enlightenment come. The other way is the same except that the spiritual teacher gives his follower a question. Both sit together thinking of the question: "What is my permanent state of mind?" or "How do I comprehend a sound or a flash of light?" These questions seem to have no meaning; no hint for any solution is given. But the answer lies in an experience of value. The answer is never a verbal answer. The answer is expressed in an attitude of the whole body. We become like a lower animal, with no concepts and with no speech. The answer is not with the mouth, but in conduct, in action. In other words, speech and concepts are always false; we need a direct experience. We do not understand, but we become our self. As we should describe this state in the speech of our laboratories, we inhibit all particular concepts; attention is so widely distributed that all special ideas are kept subconscious, yet the mind is kept in an intense tension-feeling. In this state the mind is ready to respond to any suggested stimulus lofty enough in quality to excite it. It is calm, but full of latent power.

This state of mind is precisely the opposite of the mind which the West is struggling to form. The East is firmly convinced that the mind not directed to objects is the true state of mind. The West is beginning to believe that the mind is a series of more or less dissociated sensations. But may not both be true? May not both be relative points of view? Are not both subject and object artificial classifications of pure experience? Neither can exist without the other. Sometimes one and sometimes the other attracts more attention. But we may cultivate either; we may give our lives to an approach to one or to the other extremity of experience. We may try to make ourselves sure of subjective categorical imperatives and of logics of mathematics with no regard to particular existing objects; or we may lose ourselves altogether in the contemplation of objects of beauty; or we may struggle to transcend both subject and object in a pure experience.

It is not true, then, that mysticism must deny the existence of objects, the existence of persons or of things. But it does deny that there can be a personality, in the highest sense of the word and on the highest levels of reality, unless there be one inclusive system of values or one will which is complete in itself, and a single system of ideas expressing this will or value.

If any person's values are changeable, if desires are constantly sifting through each other, that person cannot accomplish much of a result because of the weakness of his motives. Or again, if his system of concepts does not work well, the range of thoughts narrows, the person is moved all the time by one exclusive set of impulses, and his interests become infantile. But as the desires become refined and more comprehensive, the personality becomes less intermittent. The man is now no longer satisfied with helping one set of desires by mutilating others which he equally values. He tries to give satisfaction to all; and he adds new values of beauty, of ethics, of social life. Still even these higher levels of personality may waver; the passion for art may cease; the chivalrous instinct may come too late; unforeseen self-centred desires may flicker up within him. Then it is that the mystic presses on, intent upon the one eternal system of beliefs expressed in one concept which shall subordinate all these spasmodic interests, which shall include all values within itself, and which shall order all in such wise that good shall not clash with good. Whatever the path be to the mystic's goal,—whether it be in the life of the forest, or in the voice of swaying trees; whether it be Gautama's Nirvana stilling the body and mind in an ecstasy of keen intelligence; or whether it be the path of Francis of Assisi, wooing poverty as his bride and serving her by finding the one meaning of life in lowly forms, in birds, in wolves and lepers, in rich men and in thieves,—do we not feel that in our harsh and greedy modern life we have lost something which these tireless wandering dreamers found, and are we not the poorer when they take to their path again and leave us, with our machinery and our possessions and our piled-up furniture, feeling vulgar and needy and wondering through what ages of striving we must pass before we can approach their simplicity?

This problem still remains upon our hands: how we can feel sure of this one supreme value in all life, and at the same time be true to the social loyalties and to the collective beliefs which we are hourly striving to express in definite deeds.

LECTURE SIXTH

VI

LEVELS OF RELIGION

ANY attempt to estimate in what respect one religion is complete, and another not complete, must come at the end and not at the beginning of the discussion. The complete religion could not be a new religion: there is no such religion. Still less is it a philosopher's religion or the religion of any band of specialists. Such religions are traceable in the past; but soon their place knows them no more. The complete religion must be far more comprehensive. Every one who has breathed the breath of life and felt its mystery and desired its fulness knows in his own experience what religion is. Neither the vagueness of the experience nor the endless variety of its forms affects the fact that the experience is direct and universal. It is then less important exactly to limit the definition of complete religion than to make sure that no characteristic level of religious experience is omitted.

In a complete religion we should distinguish the characteristic features and take care only that we do not exchange theological, or philosophical, or any other ready-made conceptual substitutes for the actual expansion of religious life. The completeness would consist in a constant extension of life; and this life must be effective on at least three levels of experience.

A religion of any vitality at all must include, on its first level, a vivid and inner feeling of personal values. Beliefs as the expressions of values, and ideas as portrayals of beliefs, must not be substituted for the values themselves. There need be no clear idea, unless there be an attempt to communicate the value. But in every religion there must be the characteristic personal thrill of expectation, of wonder, of surprise, of enthusiasm which is what is called religious emotion.

The second level, of quite a different quality, consists of collective values and must find expression in social forms of life. In a complete religion the sense of correspondence between the two levels is a spontaneous feeling of a discovery of more life; each level falls into its new place and each strengthens the texture of the other. But in lower religions the first level of unconscious and impulsive life is easily concealed under the conceptual and voluntary life of the second level of the social life. In such religions the superficial social layer, trained not to react to outer excitements, floats insecurely upon the stagnant unconscious personal life, the deeper and animal level, still fluctuating with primitive conditions of life. A primitive religion expresses and discovers these rudimentary impulses and buries them under the weight of social usages and of verbal substitutions. But under the stress of conflicting impulses the correspondence is broken, the religion is rent, the upper layer of speech and custom is stripped off, and the animal man stands forth again alone.

The third level of values is a system of supersensible realities. This level is a metaphysical level; and the metaphysics is very often mysticism. This level of religion moves in a kind of being which is not confined to groups of men or to things that men can touch or see or feel. Knowledge on this level insists that there is a kind of being which does not exist in its totality at any one moment of time, and is not in its totality at any point of space or in any part of Nature. In that sense it does not exist; just as number cannot exist as a magnitude or as an object of perception. The objects of this level of religion cannot exist as objects of perception, and yet they are.

Normative judgements are of this kind of being; and these objects which cannot be perceived correspond to the best attainable system of actual human purposes. This system of normative purposes controls the inhibitions and impulses of life. It is a constant background for every dramatic advance. And it raises and expands the whole life. No universal religion has failed to insist upon such a system of supersensible realities and to teach that the value of these realities is universal. The value is universal in the sense that some such system is obligatory upon every right-thinking man, and in the sense that it corresponds to what each man and each society wishes most consistently for itself. Each of the universal religions is an attempt to adjust our personal life to these supersensible realities, to perfect constantly the sense of direction towards them, and to make men feel that there is nothing in our lives that is out of relation to them.

The three levels, personal and social and metaphysical, correspond in a numberless variety of combinations. The interest lies in the correspondence of the personal life and of the social life with the higher universal level. It is in the peculiar character of this correspondence that the completeness of a religion must consist. Religion, in the full sense, is the life on this highest level, the life in the Normal Consciousness, the life which is not the product of the individual nor of the race nor of empirical conditions.

On the metaphysical level there are three great religions: ascetic mysticism, social mysticism, and historical mysticism. An example of the first would be the Vedanta system, an example of the second would be Buddhism, and Christianity would be the third.

The first of these types, ascetic mysticism, is not a permanent state of ecstasy; it is a development culminating in one supreme insight. It is a life ordered in a single direction towards one idea. Mysticism differs from any other deliberate pursuit of one fixed aim only in one respect: in the character of the culmination at which it aims. The different stages may coincide with levels of ordinary life. But the final stage is the essential feature: this is ecstasy. Ecstasy is such a narrowing of the stream of consciousness that outer objects are inhibited, and is at the same time a concentration of the stream upon one idea of great dignity. The point of departure is an aspiration after a supersensible being of absolute perfection. The perfect being is as yet unknown and unrepresentable in knowledge. But the search for it besets the whole inner life until the concept appears as the concrete expression of fulfilled aspiration and the counterpart of human needs. Life is interpreted in terms of perfection. A divine ideal draws men upward to itself. The thought of God logically precedes all self-seeking motives. All imperfect ideas merge in the one perfect being; all partial acts of will surcharge God with their own authority.

Thus the mystic's world is inverted. The old world loses its fascination; its colour pales; admiration for the old system of values becomes meaningless and painful. All is now focal upon a higher level. The old ideal is faded and dead; and before the mind rises the perfect being, the final expression of all the expectations and strivings of past life, now, at last, an ideal living within the inmost self, — and so perfect that no perceptible reality can express what it contains. All things are now seen to be fragments of one unlimited whole. One word implies within itself all possible meanings; one concept is the sole object of desire; one substance owns all possible properties. And this energized within the mystic when as yet he knew it not. In the words of the great Vedantist, "This is his real form, in which his wishes are fulfilled, in which the Self only is his wish, in which no wish is left. There is then no second, no other different from him that he could see."

At this point the ascetic mystic diverges sharply from the Buddhist and the Christian. The one Being alone is worthy. Methodically the ascetic begins to strip off the ties which bind him to his fellows, bind him to objects formerly loved,—all feelings must conform to the One. Consequently internal combat against social loyalties is encouraged. The tension-feeling increases the determination to cut the bond. There must be abrupt change; there must be no transitory values; there must be changeless being in perfect purity. All shall be of the quality of the ecstasy, of immediate experience with no associative memories or desires. The self is in the perfect being and it is in the self. The self is total being and itself at the same time. The feeling of contrast of personality to personality is lost. There must be no social level whatsoever. The only value is above; the only progress is from above; the perfect must create in us the search for itself; nothing not perfect has any value. The only relation in life is self-identity; the only aim is the effort to be perfect. The life of the world is a hindrance. Henceforth the ascetic devotes himself to contemplation; henceforth let no man know him; henceforth he is a passenger on earth.

This mysticism unifies and coördinates all values in a single concrete experience. This experience is as clear to this mystic as is the taste of pineapple or as the colour of the hibiscus. The quality is different, but the experience not less vivid; on the contrary he insists it is more specific. All mystics know that the personal life inheres in an infinite system of supersensible reality. The ascetic mystic differs from others in his way of approach to this metaphysical being. The rigid mystic of this type is convinced that the only method of approach is to abolish this world. Social life is renounced; family, state and property, art and science must cease utterly to prevail. There can be no middle term between the One and the individual soul. Human societies and human loyalties are illusory and must be suppressed. All is repressed except the Great Self.

This programme cannot easily be completed; the actual result is often nothing more than the establishment of a correspondence between the old primitive level of the animal instinct of self-preservation and the new level of ecstatic aspiration. In the words of Spinoza, "The passion to be perfect is the same as the tendency to persist in one's own form of being."

The social type of mystic, such as Gautama, has a similar system of control for life: he also, by means of a symbolic idea of perfect experience, attempts to feel that experience. For him also there is no external, no transcendence; all is internal, all is continuous, all is limitless; there is no contrast of mind or body, of subject and object, nor any such thing; all is a unique Presence supertemporal and free and self-determined; all is life; all is self; all is peace.

The ineffable union summing up in one all known values is concretely experienced. When the mystic's self merges, on the higher level, in the one perfect meaning, the sting of defeat is soothed away in passionate adoration. His life yields him pleasure of hitherto undreamed purity. His exaltation in his own self with beautiful precision unifies his life. All his aspirations for the ideal find their counterpart in his own experience. This sense of correspondence is the source of his delight. The inner anarchy is now transformed into a single order. The one idea, absolute in the authority of its beauty, persists in consciousness without perceptible change, and so directs the stream of thoughts that emotional tones and motor tendencies fall automatically into correspondence with it. This exceptional unification of the stream of consciousness diffuses him with joy and focuses his will in mighty moral efforts.

This mystic of this joyous and social type finds his highest value of life not in hatred of the world of change, not in disgust at men and at human institutions and at social aims, but in an almost ecstatic delight in contemplating them all. After their ecstasies these mystics look again at the life of men, the ordinary life in the fields or in the lanes of the city, and it appears to them transfigured. To the pure all things are pure. The poor human animal is evil only when gazed upon with carnal eye. In loving the despised and the rejected this mystic finds his peace and loves his God. To find the new value in the old life is to him a test of courage, a trial of strength and skill, a spiritual athletics, a knightly exercise. Every limb, every impulse, every faculty, shall be at the bidding of the one supreme value. Thus his life is to him a kind of practice for the higher intensities of soul. He chooses to taste pain, he searches for pain; he makes the world a part of himself, and himself a part of the one life. Other men are not felt to be distinct from himself. And in hearing all living hearts beat in correspondence with his own pulsating feelings, he has his reward: a sublime sense of correspondence with the highest level. As Gautama would put it, "By ceasing to hunt for pleasures and by ceasing to fear pain, by the cessation of the conditions for both, and by concentration of mind, the lesser values have no meaning,—thus only, and on an immense scale, we gain the real, the unchanging, the peace."

In Buddhism, then, concentration of mind, implying a withdrawal from the world, is of fundamental importance. Accompanying this is an extraordinary interest in ordinary social life. Both mystical and social levels seem complete: Buddhism has duties and privileges for both recluse and householder. There is no thought of abolishing social loyalties; both social loyalties and mystical ideals coexist in the same religion. But while both are recognized, the ascetic life is looked upon not only as the highest, but as absolutely essential to the highest result. We read that

Nagasena taught the king Milinda, who questioned him on this very matter, that no person "can enter the path that leads to peace" who has not observed the thirteen ordinances, that is, who has not embraced the monastic life in the present birth or in a former birth. Faithful householders could be born into heaven; Nirvana was reached only by the ascetic life.

This ascetic ideal will of course affect the whole conception of loyalty and of duty. If the ascetic life is regarded as the normal life, and if the values of life are estimated according as they bring a man nearer this ideal standard; the ordinary level has a morbid element injected into it which must affect all its ramifications. The morality of Buddhism is of a very high standard; we do honour to its sublimity and to its beauty; but it is not easy to overlook this morbid element. Effective life depends upon the clearness and accuracy of the moral will. If this is confused, the whole inner world of values will suffer. And confusion results as truly from over-strictness as from laxity. If a man believes that what is in itself indifferent is either duty or crime, the poise of will is injured as truly, though perhaps not so decisively, as though what in itself is wrong is made to appear right. At least the balance is disturbed. The morbid view of life which underlies the Buddhist mystical ideal introduces into the standards of life the results which we should thus expect. This effect is aggravated by that other view of life which makes a deed chiefly valuable as it contributes to the spiritual advancement of the individual doing it. Thus we have in the Buddhist morality often a certain extravagant, morbid, and we are tempted to say, maudlin character which we cannot help noticing even while we admire the extraordinary elevation of the standard. This element may be illustrated by a description of one of the meditations practised by the Buddha: "Then, Ananda, the Great King of Glory went out from the chamber of the Great Complex and entered the Golden Chamber and sat himself down on the golden couch. And he let his mind pervade one quarter of the world with thoughts of Love; and so the second quarter, and so the third, and so the fourth. And thus the whole wide world, above, below, around, and everywhere, did he continue to pervade with heart of Love, far-reaching, grown great, and beyond measure, free from the least trace of anger or ill-will." This process was repeated with thoughts of Pity, then with thoughts of Sympathy, and finally with thoughts of Equanimity. Later this exercise became one of the practices required of Buddhist monks. When the monk had arrived at a convenient spot and placed himself in a proper position, he was to exercise this wish, "May all the superior orders of beings be happy; may all men, whether they be monks or laymen, all the devas, all who are suffering the pains of hell, be happy; may they be free from sorrow, disease, and evil desire."

From the Buddhist point of view, which makes the culture of the inner sense of being and the freedom of the individual from all outward bonds the most decisive aims, this meditation has its place and its meaning. But to Western minds it seems neither a preparation for social service nor anything like a prayer, but more like an aimless overflowing towards space, a kind of ungrounded happiness and good-fellowship with the universe; consequently to us it appears somewhat extravagant. The same boundlessness we discover in the acts of charity for which the Buddha is praised: in former states of existence he had given away everything. To us this ideal of conduct seems aimless, unbalanced and sentimental. It is easy to see the value of such acts as elements in the discipline of one who is trying to sever all the ties which bind him to the earth; but giving to one who asks until he is loaded with gifts that he needs less than the giver while the rights of others are ignored, has small social value.

While we consider these blemishes in the otherwise almost perfect system of Buddhist morality, it is well not to forget that in contrast to this exaggerated self-discipline, we have in the life of the Buddha himself an example of sublime self-sacrifice. Out of pure unselfishness, out of the devotion of love and pity, he lavished his life upon the world. This life goes far to counteract the imperfect social morality. And in Japan this defect is supplemented by the intense social loyalties of the Shinto religion to the state and to the family ideal; the result to-day is the very highest quality of social morality.

The third type of religion on the metaphysical level is the Christian religion. If we consider the early Christian religion wherever it has manifested itself in its original purity, it is sharply contrasted with the ideal life of ascetic mysticism or with the ideal life of Buddhism. Christianity asserts the value of the personal life, with its concrete rights and its obligations and its needs as the chief end of the final purpose of the world. Human lives are not to be abolished; human wills are not to be absorbed in one mass of absolutely identical experience. All men are to seek life together; each life is to give all it can to the other lives; the past is to give life to the present, the present is to correct the errors of the past; all men are to will one common purpose. This purpose, constantly developing and endlessly fulfilling itself, is the one supersensible reality running through all human lives: to know this is eternal life. No one fulfils this one will which unifies all lives; nor do all working together as parts of one collective purpose know its full meaning; it is beyond all and yet in all; and each one is this purpose, so far as he can will it. All this is an entire change of emphasis: God is not rigid, changeless, infinite rapture, consisting of the perfect thought of self; nor is He the last and the most impersonal abstraction of actual experience. But God is the ultimate energy of personal will, not dependent on any one human will nor upon any social will, and yet inseparable from any human will, and necessarily conditioning every will. The contemplative ideal gives place to that of action, to the unflinching, practical fulfilment, by persons and by social units, of one endless purpose. Men are not to reflect what they are, but to will to become what they are capable of being. The end of life is the realization by each man of his own capacities. These capacities may be regarded as elements of one infinite purpose; this purpose needs our lives and carries them to one common goal which is altogether beyond our efforts to reach or even to conceive. This realization cannot be effected by a variety of impulses, nor by meditation upon abstract ideals, but only by an increasing sequence and ordering of purposes toward a common, infinite goal, by virtue of a feeling of internal obligation of will, a feeling that a man owes more to himself than any one impulse can give. Loyalties toward other men are a part of a man's own purpose for himself, and each purpose, so far as each man wills it, is defined by its place in the one plan. And so far as effort to live out the one common loyalty in deeds is tested by pain, the more clearly the quality of the one common life becomes purified within us and fixed in the focus of our voluntary life.

All these abstractions were portrayed by Christ in descriptions of the search for the Kingdom of God and His righteousness. The quality of this kingdom of souls, of the nature of God, and of His righteousness are identical. All are aspects of the same thing from different points of view. The kingdom is the social level, or in the later theological language, the Spirit. Life in this kingdom is the gift of God, is the revelation to us of Ultimate Being; He is the Giver of all good things, or in the later theological language, the Father. The righteousness is the personal sense of correspondence to these other levels. All three express one purpose; all three are one in quality and aim. The metaphysical level is meaningless, if out of correspondence with the social. The social level has meaning in itself, but the ideal of a common life, which consists of human beings, those who choose to will the higher purposes of other lives as the final purpose of their own lives, a kingdom founded on ideal human love,—this has wider and more permanent significance than the mutual relations of men to each other. The ability to will such an ideal, and the ability to think of the world with reference to such an ideal, becomes the critical experience. Science and art and politics and economics may all be counted as particular expressions of one infinite purpose, in which each life of the past, each one of ourselves and of the races to come, has his definite opportunity, at a definite point, to share. The sense of working out such a mighty purpose in one's own life gives a man the right mettle to face the world; in contrast to this the ascetic ideal seems more a cry of defeat from men of weaker moral fibre, an appeal for a tenderer humanity, an entreaty for a more merciful and peaceful world.

One of the unique qualities in Christianity is that this metaphysical ideal becomes the single aim of the historical life of Christ, who gave his whole life to the training of a band of men who should communicate this ideal by personal contact with single individuals to the race of men. The choice of that task as a life-calling, the foundation in history of a spiritual kingdom based upon the belief that we count most to ourselves when we choose the lives of others as expressions of our own life, and at the same time as expressions of the Ultimate Will, is not superseded by other ideals.

The peculiar effectiveness of this life of Christ seems due to a certain elemental simplicity and candour which makes him an absolute master of himself, and makes his revelation of God inseparable from his own inner life.

Absolute certainty is the commonest form of belief, especially for the lower grades of mentality and the lower forms of religion. As soon as comparisons and reformations seem inevitable, the original absolute certitude becomes a scientific certitude; reality is thought in general terms of serial order and not in isolated terms of absolute impression. However much legendary material and theological speculation obscure from us the character of Christ, it is evident that his religious insight into reality was unfaltering in its order and unobscured in its range of aim. His life was not a partial life, wavering with the ambitions of struggling men, but rather life in the absolute consciousness; not only over-individual, but over-social and over-empirical. Certainty of this consciousness is absolute: never the certainty of momentary excitement, and not the belief in the reality of our ideals, but the firm conviction of the supremacy of the final purpose of reality in us. Every act seems an expression of this purpose that the total life of man on all its levels shall be brought into a feeling of correspondence with the absolute will: and of the belief that the absolute will, in its breadth, in its height and depths, is in close correspondence with each personal life and is a constant standard of desire for all lives, and that there is yet no end to the variation of its relations to single personal lives. The resulting history, so far as we can trace, has been that the religion of Christ has absorbed within itself a richer deposit from all other beliefs than any other religion; that it has drawn into itself numberless streams of personal desire, of aesthetical taste, of social inventions and of mystical systems,—all of which have been the life of the most cultivated races. The appeal has been not to authority nor to reason, but to conscience, aesthetic or social or mystical. And thus, this Man, although using power drawn neither from economics nor from politics nor from church, nor from science or art, was so penetrated with passionate love of men and of the Father-God, and so true to each man's own best wishes for his own good, that whenever the inner motives of His life have been understood, the enlightened conscience of humanity has accepted Him as representative of the religious conscience of the race, and has followed His life and found Life in Him.